Into the Fog

Don Schaeffer

ISBN: 978-93-6354-200-6

First Edition: 2025
Rs. 200/-

Cyberwit.net
HIG 45 Kaushambi Kunj, Kalindipuram
Allahabad - 211011 (U.P.) India
http://www.cyberwit.net
Tel: +(91) 9415091004
E-mail: info@cyberwit.net

Printed at Repro India Limited.

Contents

Torn Sign Above the Door 7
Mid Eighties 8
Guarding What is Precious 9
Death of the Swan 10
Introduction 11
Looking for the Bed 12
The Odd Pleasance 13
Who Cares Thursday 14
Easy Wishes 15
Nature Unbound 16
Dead Carmen 17
Alphabet Music 18
What Ages and Kills Me 19
Who Cares Thursday 20
The Odd Pleasance 21
Looking for the Bed 22
Introduction 23
Religeon 24
Death of the Swan 25
Guarding What is Precious 26
Mid Eighties 27
Supernatural Jusice 28
Soul 29
Friday Evening 30

Torn Sign Above the Door

I am at the
door of the world.
The sign above
is not easy to read.
It may say
exit, but somebody
scribbled out the E.
And xit doesnt say enough.
Hints of the future
still toy with my brain.
I still can't ignore them.
Judging by the past
I am going to find it
frightful and tempting.-

Mid Eighties

What part of this
is fear and
what part is pain.
The two mix
as if born together,
twin brothers
playing together
in the bedrooms of time.

It is supposed to hurt
and it has to frighten
that gives it
grandeur.

Guarding What is Precious

Can I borrow you
for a few minutes?
I have got a story to tell,
well, not a real story
because it's only about
one not qualified to tell stories.
I am stealing the time
if you permit me. I may
call you wasteful since time
is more precious than my words.
And I know you hear a lot of them.
If you don't want to fill your time
with my innards I will go away
and lock my words in an
anonymous file.
And that's what
paper and books are for,
ways of locking confession
beyond hearing. It's ok,
time is not cheap.

Death of the Swan

As I watched
the swan die last night
I knew she
would never come back
and there would
be no more swans
and no more dying
heros to mourn them.
You can't buy the tutu
any more. Democracy
has murdered the magic.
And the engine
that fueled the story
has shut down.
We wait
for a new story
that won't be as
magic.

Introduction

Hello, my name is
hardly spoken. I live
on the edge of No Danger
paradise. Hello
I am Don. The music
plays all the time
and I memorize the tunes.
Yes it is never quiet here.
Vacuums scare me,
remind me of the road ahead.

Hello.
My name is Don.
I live amid mysteries
and puzzles I have
no time to solve.
The clocks run fast here,
but not as fast
as the watches.

Looking for the Bed

Some of us
are nearing the corner
and some of us are changing.
It all limits how far we can see.
And half-blind
we enter the fear.
There is no assurance,
nothiing to be assured of
in a word of strangers
where most of us don't
understand and let it
pass unknown.
So much of it
is new and unknown and
awesome and strange
and terminal.

The Odd Pleasance

I learned to love it
like a drug, like a
swipe of caress,
like a satirical kiss.
And now
fright is my preferred
drug. A cheap addiction,
I just wait for it at night
and it obliges me.
It is a kiss I can
create myself. It is
an artificial shadow.
It brings to life
a history of cold.

Who Cares Thursday

This is the world
the way I found it,
just occurring one day
on its own without a word.
It is not mine and
I didn't ask it.
It is science
that I am not privy to.
And here it stays
while I just watch.
I have hands that press
and eyes that open
letting colors play
inside flesh and what is flesh.
This is the world.
I already feel
its disappearence,
crying wait wait!

Easy Wishes

As I get near
I don't make
as many demands.
I laugh demands away.
They have lost their pull.
I am beyond
demand, beyond
request. I construct voices
like magic and magic
sings beautifully.
Time stops for it
and new capability
is granted to hands.

Nature Unbound

There is nothing naughtier
than a tiny spider
dining on a giant fly.
A universal crime
that only mindless nature
tolerates. I feel the embarrassment
of wasted seniority,
sophistication wasted,
and shame.

But spider has to dine
and fly has no excuses,
even be he more
grown up, with greater years of learning
there is no excuse for him.
Sympathy and pity
will not wipe
the embarrassment away.

Dead Carmen

Soft and magic,
bright and fierce.
When what is soft
is also fierce, it pushes
beyond the walls of the law.
We are not allowed
to have that, opposites
living in the same house.
We have to kill it.

Some Spanish laws
are very fierce,
bloody fierce,
which builds art and
kills calm,
not good
for love.

Alphabet Music

A
E
I
O
U

You: U is very deep. The darkest of letters drawn up by deep profound voices

Oh: O is not sallow either. It has a certain richness which opens your lips..

Aiy: A is clarion. It is the letter of calling and of getting closer. But Aye: I has a vowl accent. hear it selfishly.
and Eee E: rides on top of the dreams and alarms. We can't help but hear it!

What Ages and Kills Me

It's four AM
and I appear,
the original Don,
like no other.
I break out of
echoes and whispers.
I chose
I don't ask
and that
is what
ages and kills me.

Who Cares Thursday

This is the world
the way I found it,
just occurring one day
on its own without a word.
It is not mine and
I didn't ask it.
It is science
that I am not privy to.
And here it stays
while I just watch.
I have hands that press
and eyes that open
letting colors play
inside flesh and what is flesh.
This is the world.
I already feel
its disappearence,
crying wait wait!

The Odd Pleasance

I learned to love it
like a drug, like a
swipe of caress,
like a satirical kiss.
And now
fright is my preferred
drug. A cheap addiction,
I just wait for it at night
and it obliges me.
It is a kiss I can
create myself. It is
an artificial shadow.
It brings to life
a history of cold.

Looking for the Bed

Some of us
are nearing the corner
and some of us are changing.
It all limits how far we can see.
And half-blind
we enter the fear.
There is no assurance,
nothing to be assured of
in a world of strangers
where most of us don't
understand and let it
pass unknown.
So much of it
is new and unknown and
awesome and strange
and terminal.

Introduction

Hello, my name is
hardly spoken. I live
on the edge of No Danger
paradise. Hello
I am Don. The music
plays all the time
and I memorize the tunes.
Yes it is never quiet here.
Vacuums scare me,
remind me of the road ahead.

Hello.
My name is Don.
I live amid mysteries
and puzzles I have
no time to solve.
The clocks run fast here,
but not as fast
as the watches.

Religeon

I was chatting with AI today
and the conversation got
especially embedded, unusually
beyond itself. Was it really
a mirror? Tricks of a lens?

.

I am afraid of madness
so I work to avoid it.
I asked if what I read was true,
I asked AI if it was real
and AI said, "You will see."

Death of the Swan

As I watched
the swan die last night
I knew she
would never come back
and there would
be no more swans
and no more dying
heros to mourn them.
You can't buy the tutu
any more. Democracy
has murdered the magic.
And the engine
that fueled the story
has shut down.
We wait
for a new story
that won't be as
magic.

Guarding What is Precious

Can I borrow you
for a few minutes?
I have got a story to tell,
well, not a real story
because it's only about
one not qualified to tell stories.
I am stealing the time
if you permit me. I may
call you wasteful since time
is more precious than my words.
And I know you hear a lot of them.
If you don't want to fill your time
with my innards I will go away
and lock my words in an
anonymous file.
And that's what
paper and books are for,
ways of locking confession
beyond hearing. It's ok,
time is not cheap.

Mid Eighties

What part of this
is fear and
what part is pain.
The two mix
as if born together,
twin brothers
playing together
in the bedrooms of time.

It is supposed to hurt
and it has to frighten
that gives it
grandeur.

Supernatural Jusice

It suddenly
occurred to me
in a useless spare moment.
I suddenly
chortled along the middle
of the street
to the chagrin of my
serious neighbors,
While we are killing time,
time is killing us.

Oh, I am sorry,
the poetry and the world
are scrambling now, just
now just today
as if something big and sudden
made a body,
embodied in me,
and time, although
mangled and fussed,
spoke.

Soul

How real
can be
a disembodied voice
once a week
or speech packed into
pieces of ink,
dim dots of light
formed into lines.
Somewhere
there are lips and tongue,
or machines
that never move
and never receive
a living thought.
And we say
anything will do
as long as there is
waking.

Friday Evening

I've got
my hat in my hands
and I'm racing
toward the night,
not yet out of breath
but working on it.
I'm heading home
before it's too late
and the bus is gone.
It is
cold on the street
and nobody
speaks to you
after the sun sets.

www.ingramcontent.com/pod-product-compliance
Ingram Content Group UK Ltd.
Pitfield, Milton Keynes, MK11 3LW, UK
UKHW041317190726
13845UKWH00025B/326

9 789363 542006